Backyard Scientist®

Series Four

by Jane Hoffman

Illustrated by Lanny Ostroff

The Backyard Scientist series includes:

"The Original Backyard Scientist." This widely read and popular book was the author's first writing effort and features many of her most popular experiments for children ages 4 through 12 years. **"Backyard Scientist, Series One."** The author's second book of science experiments provides children ages 4 through 12 with more fascinating and fun ways to explore the world of science. **"Backyard Scientist, Series Two,"** is the writer's third book. It is geared for children ages 9 through 14 years and features a special collection of exciting, fascinating and challenging experiments. **"Backyard Scientist, Series Three,"** teaches young scientists ages 4 through 12 about the living world with experiments in biology, physiology, entomology and more.

Backyard Scientist, Series Four
Spring 1992
Library of Congress catalog number: 91-092390
Published by Backyard Scientist/Jane Hoffman
P. O. Box 16966
Irvine, CA 92713
©1992 by Backyard Scientist/Jane Hoffman

0-9618663-4-9

The Subject Matter of this book is based on the scientific. The author is specific in directions, explanations and warnings. If what is written is disregarded, failure or complication may occur - just as in the case in the laboratory. In the instances where flammable or toxic chemicals are involved, explicit explanation and warnings are provided.

TABLE OF CONTENTS

Experiment	Page#

THE REVIEWS ARE IN ON BACKYARD SCIENTIST
WHAT EDUCATORS AND PARENTS ARE SAYING ABOUT THE BACKYARD SCIENTIST

"For the easiest and most enjoyable approach to science experiments, I recommend (The Backyard Scientist) by Jane Hoffman"

-- Mary Pride
The Teaching Home

"Her goal (is) to see the public school system adopt an ongoing, daily, hands-on science curriculum. No one can say that Jane Hoffman isn't doing her part to try to achieve this aim."

-- Nita Kurmins Gilson
The Christian Science Monitor

("Hoffman's) own curiosity and energy are a large part of the appeal of The Backyard Scientist. 'I believe that science makes a difference in the way a child learns.'"

--The Chicago Tribune

"Anyone who can read, or get an assistant to read, can have fun building the experiments described in The Backyard Scientist series and then have even more fun using (Hoffman's) experiments to explore science."

-- Paul Doherty, Ph.D.
Physicist/Teacher

"What makes these experiments special is their hands-on nature. A firm believer that science makes a difference in how a child learns, Hoffman encourages kids to think for themselves, to ask questions and to observe the world around them."

-- Science Books and Films

"All of the experiments have been pre-tested extensively with groups of children."

-- Curriculum Product News Magazine

"I believe that you have many of the answers to our problems with science education in the early grades."

~ Mary Kohleman
National Science Foundation
Washington, DC

"There are a lot of good reasons why you should order the books, but if you need another one, just remember you're doing it for a worthy cause--your students."

--Teaching K-8 Magazine

"Popcorn, ice cubes and string are among the materials used in her experiments...most of which the children conduct themselves. But the main ingredient is the enthusiasm that Jane generates in the fledgling scientistsl."

-- Women's Day Magazine

"...(Backyard Scientist series) is the best 'hands-on' experience a young reader can help him or herself to. Original and highly recommended for schools and home-teaching."

-- Children's Bookwatch

"As a teacher, I truly appreciated your book. It was well organized and easy to follow. The experience with a variety of scientific concepts has sparked further interest in several areas with many of the students. They have asked for more!"

-- Amy Korenack
Resource Teacher

"She•makes science come alive."

-- Orange Coast Daily Pilot

"Backyard Scientest teaches children the art of thinking."

-- Anaheim Bulletin

"My mom is a teacher and thinks these books are the greatest"

-- Ryan, Age 5

"I loved the 'Backyard Scientist Series.' I like things I hadn't thought of doing by myself."

-- Chris, Age 7

"I loved the 'Backyard Scientist' books. They are so great."

- Thomas Age 8-1/2

"I tried your experiments with my students and they went wild with excitement."

-- First Grade Teacher, Illinois

"I really appreciate the clear instructions, simple to get household supplies, and the complete and easy to understand explanations. Thanks for these wonderful books."

-- Mrs. Getz, Home Schooling Mom

Welcome to the intriguing, mystifying and stimulating Backyard Scientist Laboratory. The laboratory features hands-on science experiments. Performing the experiments in this book will enhance your critical thinking skills and expose you to the fun and interesting world of scientific explorations. The experiments, while designed to be simple to perform, represent complex scientific principles to which we are exposed in our daily lives.

As soon as you begin experimenting, you become a *Backyard Scientist* working in the real world of scientific investigation. Your laboratory is wherever you are experimenting, be it in your backyard, kitchen or basement.

As Backyard Scientists working in your laboratories, there are some very important guidelines you must follow:

1. **Always** work with an adult.
2. **Never** taste anything you are experimenting with except when instructed to do so in the experiment.
3. **Always** follow the Backyard Scientist directions in the experiment.
4. **Always** wash your hands with soap and warm water after you finish experimenting.
5. **Be a patient** scientist. Some experiments take longer than others before results can be observed.
6. **Some experiments in this book use household chemicals that are poisons if swallowed. I have included cautions at the beginning of all experiments in which these types of chemicals are used.**
7. If you have any questions about any of the experiments, write to me, Jane Hoffman, The Backyard Scientist, P.O. Box 16966, Irvine, CA 92713.

You are ready to start experimenting. Have fun!

Happy Experimenting,

Jane Hoffman

Your Friend,
Jane Hoffman,
The Backyard Scientist

The Backyard Scientist series of books could not continue to grow without the help of Jason, my son and the support of my husband, Arnold. And many thanks go to Sid and Grace Goldsmith, my parents, who provide the additional encouragement to continue the work. I also want to thank the many other special people who have helped through the years. They know who they are.

Additional thanks go to the tens of thousands of people who have purchased the other Backyard Scientist books.

Realizing there is more that needs to be done to help children develop their interest in science, and to remove some of the burden of teaching science in schools, I am helping teachers learn about hands-on science instruction through Backyard Scientist teacher in-service workshops. Teachers learn science basics, receive exciting resource materials, learn hands-on methods, and build self-confidence to use the hands-on approach in the classroom. Special workshops are offered to interested parent groups.

Can you clean a copper penny using electricity?

Try the following Backyard Scientist experiment to discover the answer.

ADULT SUPERVISION IS REQUIRED ON THIS EXPERIMENT.

Gather the following supplies:

One 6 volt lantern battery, two 12" or 14" lengths of copper wire, 2 small alligator clips (available at hardware and Radio Shack stores), 1 tsp. salt (non-iodized works best), 2 or more dirty copper pennies, copper cleaning polish, a spoon, paper towels, a small (4 or 6 oz.) plastic cup, and 1 cup water, a pair of scissors and a small screwdriver.

Start Experimenting:

1. Fill the plastic cup with water. Add one teaspoon of salt to the water and stir until all the salt is dissolved.
2. Remove about 1" of the insulation from each end of the wires (have an adult help you). Attach an alligator clip to one end of each of the two copper wires. Connect one of the wires to the positive terminal of the battery and the other wire to the negative terminal.

NEVER TOUCH THE OTHER TWO ENDS TOGETHER, AS IT WILL CAUSE A SHORT CIRCUIT.

3. Clip a tarnished penny to the alligator clip connected to the positive battery terminal. Attach it as close to the edge of the penny as possible.

4. Now place this and the other wire, with the clip, into the salt solution. Make sure the alligator clip, which holds the penny, goes into the solution just far enough to cover the entire penny.
5. Observe very carefully what is taking place in the cup for the next five to six minutes.

Before going on to the next step, can you answer the following questions from your observations?

1. Did you notice the bubbles coming from this process?
2. Do you know what kind of gas made these bubbles?
3. What color did your solution change into?
4. What is the cause of this new color?
5. Were the bubbles coming from the wire attached to the negative terminal or from the wire attached to the positive terminal?

Now continue experimenting.

6. Take the penny out of the salt solution, rinse it in clean water, and pat it dry with a paper towel. Take the second dirty penny and clean it with some copper cleaning polish following the directions on its container.
7. Observe very carefully the differences between the pennies.

Can you answer the following additional questions from your observations?

1. Which penny is brighter and why?
2. What does the copper cleaner contain that the electrical cleaning method does not?

3. What would happen if you used a metal cup in which to perform this experiment? Take a guess as to the answer.

Backyard Scientist solution to experiment.

When you put the penny into the salt solution, you saw bubbles coming from the negative wire. The gas causing the bubbles is hydrogen gas. The hydrogen gas causes some copper ions to be removed from the surface of the penny.

Both the electrically cleaned penny and the penny cleaned with copper cleaning polish removed the tarnish from the pennies. However, the electrically cleaned penny is dull, while the chemically cleaned penny is shiny.

When the reaction is taking place, the solution changes from clear liquid to a bluish green color. The green color is caused by the copper ions now in the solution. These, you will remember, came off the penny as the electricity flowed through the solution.

The copper cleaner contains a polishing agent that removes several layers of copper ions while the electrical method removes only the very top layer of copper ions.

You cannot use the electrical method in a metal cup, because the electricity will be short circuited to the edge of the cup. A short circuit means an unwanted flow of electricity.

Hydrogen gas is lighter than air and was used in lighter-than-air aircraft before the widespread use of helium gas. Hydrogen gas in sufficient concentrations is flammable and explosive.

Do You know how to make a mini weather station?

Try the following Backyard Scientist project.

ADULT SUPERVISION IS REQUIRED ON THIS PROJECT.

Gather the following supplies:

One wire coat hanger, four straws (straight, not the flex type), 1 or 2 empty quart size clean milk cartons, kite string, scissors, an 8 or 10 penny nail, a small paper cup, cutting pliers or a hacksaw, and a stapler.

Start Experimenting:

1. Cut off the hook of the wire hanger with the cutting pliers or hacksaw. Have an adult help you. Regular pliers will also break the wire if you bend it back and forth.
2. Bend the wire so that it makes a base with the two ends sticking up (see illustration).
3. Cut the milk carton into panels by cutting the top and bottom off, and then separate the sides. Draw two arrows on one of the side pieces of the carton. Make them exactly alike.
4. Cut out the two arrows and staple them, back to back, across the top of one of the straws.

5. Cut four strips from the milk carton about 1" x 4". Take two strips and staple them back to back at each end. Mark N on one end and S on the other end. Turn the strip over and mark N behind the original N and S behind the other S. Follow the same procedure for the other two strips and mark them E and W. Be sure both sides are the same. Slide both strips over one of the wires that are sticking up, and staple them as close to the wire as possible. Turn the strips until they form a cross with W (west) to the left of N (north).

4

6. Cut two pieces from the carton, about 1/2" x 1", and staple them onto the other wire, back to back, as above. This will act as a pivot bearing for the wind speed indicator.

7. Take one of the straws and tie it to the top of another straw (mast) with a string. It will look like a "T". To tie, loop string over the mast straw, and then bring the string ends under and over the crossing straw and tie knots.

8. Take another straw and tie it to the mast straw at a 90 degree angle to the first horizontal straw. Tie the same as in number 7 above.

9. Put the paper cup upside down on one of the carton panels and trace four circles with a pencil. Then, cut out the four circles.

10. Use the nail to punch holes into the cardboard disks you just cut. Draw a line across the center of a disk. Punch a hole 1/2" from each end on the line you have just drawn. Use this first disk as a guide, and place it on top of the other disks and punch holes in exactly the same places as the other disks, one at a time. The first disk is called a template. Bending the disks slightly will allow a straw to pass through the holes.

11. Color one cardboard disk so it looks different than the others.

12. Push one of the crossed straws through a slightly cupped cardboard disk. Install your other disks the same way.

13. You must now set the compass points. This can be done by using a small compass and lining up your north marker with it. If you do not have a compass, have someone estimate north or use the North Star in the evening to estimate north.

14. Slip the arrow over the wire with the compass pointers. Take the disk mast and put it on the wire with the pivot bearing.

15. You are now ready to test your weather station in the wind. You have just made a wind vane to find the direction of the wind and an anemometer.

Can you answer the following questions from your observations?

1. Do you know what an anemometer is?
2. How can you use your anemometer to measure wind speed?
3. Why is it useful to know from which direction the wind is blowing?

Backyard Scientist solution to experiment.

An anemometer is an instrument for measuring wind speed. The simplest anemometer works like a pinwheel. The wind spins the vanes. The number of turns it makes, in a second or minute, is recorded and translated into knots, or miles per hour. During a hurricane, wind gusts can reach 180 miles (290 km.) per hour or 160 knots, or more.

It is important to know wind direction to predict things like rainfall, moisture content of the air and so on. It is also important for airplanes taking off and landing. They usually do these by heading into the direction from which the wind is blowing.

To measure the wind speed on your anemometer, count the number of times the colored cardboard passes in front of you in a minute. Your anemometer is not accurate enough to calculate true wind speed, but you can see how fast the wind moves it. For further research into weather, you might want to go to the library and find out about the wind chill factor, barometric pressure, relative humidity, clouds, and storms. Weather is a fascinating subject to study.

Can rocks absorb and hold oil?

Try the following Backyard Scientist Experiment to discover the answer.

Gather the following supplies:

One cup cooking oil, 1 cup sand, several sheets of wax paper, an eyedropper or a straw, clay, several kinds of rock including sandstone, shale, and granite. If you don't know how to identify these, get a book on geology from the library.

Start Experimenting:

1. Spread out several sheets of wax paper on which to experiment.
2. Place 1/4 cup of sand on a sheet of wax paper.
3. With the eyedropper or straw, place four drops of oil on the sand. Carefully observe what takes place. Record your observations.
4. Place a ball of clay on another piece of wax paper.
5. Again using the eyedropper, put 4 drops of oil on the clay. Again, observe carefully. Record your observations.
6. Place the rocks on other sheets of wax paper and put four drops of oil on each. Observe very carefully. Record your observations.

Can you answer the following questions from your observations?

1. What kind of rocks can absorb and hold the oil in our experiment?
2. How can we compare these to the rocks that hold petroleum oil?
3. Do you know how different types of rocks are formed?
4. Where is coal and petroleum found?
5. What valuable products that we use every day come from petroleum?
6. Millions of years ago, remains of prehistoric animals sank to the bottom of oceans and lakes and were converted to what valuable products?
7. Can you name another fuel that is formed the same way as petroleum?
8. How long does it take for the remains of plants and animals to turn into petroleum?
9. How is petroleum made?

Backyard Scientist solution to experiment.

Did you discover that the oil was absorbed by the sand and not by the ball of clay? Depending on the other rocks you selected and used in the experiment, the oil either flowed into the pores of the rock or remained on the surface of the rock. Porous rocks such as sandstone absorbed the oil. Impervious rocks, like shale, would not absorb the oil.

Different kinds of rock are formed in different ways. In all cases pressure is a key ingredient in forming rocks. In certain kinds of rock, heat is very important (volcanic rock). In some cases, both heat and pressure are needed. For more information on rock formation, you may want to get a book on geology.

We get many valuable products from petroleum including gasoline, lubricating oil, plastics, medicines and many more. The remains of living things buried millions of years ago turned into the petroleum we use today. Another product formed the same way as petroleum, and important to heating our homes, powering electric generators, and making valuable chemicals such as chemical fertilizers and plastics, is natural gas.

Petroleum is found in pockets beneath the surface of the earth in porous sand and rocks and in underground reservoirs. It is then pumped to the surface and transported to refineries where it is converted to the valuable products we use.

When you take trips to other parts of the country, collect some small rock samples and bring them home. Repeat the experiment on them to see if they may be the kind of rock that could hold petroleum.

Can you get electricity from a lemon?

Try the following Backyard Scientist experiment to discover the answer.

ADULT SUPERVISION IS REQUIRED ON THIS EXPERIMENT. NEVER EAT OR DRINK ANYTHING YOU ARE EXPERIMENTING WITH UNLESS TOLD TO DO SO IN THE EXPERIMENT.

Gather the following supplies:

You will need 1 of the following fruits: lemon, lime, grapefruit, orange, or tangerine. You will need either an apple, pear or other non-citrus fruit; 2 lengths of insulated bell wire 14" to 20" long, 1 large steel nail, and a FM band transistor radio.

Start Experimenting:

1. Take the lemon, or one of the other citrus fruits you have chosen, and press down very hard on it. Now, roll it several times on a table. This will make it juicy inside.
2. Have an adult help you remove about 1-1/2" to 2" of the insulation from each end of the wires.
3. Take the end of one wire and tightly wrap this around the nail head. You can tape it to the nail to insure that a good contact is made.
4. Push the nail halfway into the lemon, or other citrus fruit, you are using. Push one end of the other length of wire into the fruit about 1" away from the nail. You can use the nail to punch the hole for the wire.
5. Now, take the transistor radio and place it near the lemon.
6. Turn on the FM radio and tune it between stations and put the volume on high.
7. Take one of the loose wires and touch this to the FM antenna and listen very carefully. You may do this several times.
8. Now, take both loose ends of the wires and touch them both to the FM antenna. Listen very carefully to the noise coming from the radio.
9. Take the apple, or other non-citrus fruit, and try the same experiment that you just did with your citrus fruit. Be sure to wash any residue off the nail and wire that was in the citrus fruit.

Can you answer the following questions from your observations?

1. What kind of energy are you able to get from this citrus fruit?
2. How can you compare the lemon, or the other citrus fruits, to a dry cell battery?
3. Into what have you changed the chemical energy of the citrus fruit?
4. Did you get the same results from this experiment when you used the apple or other non-citrus fruit?

Backyard Scientist solution to experiment.

Did you discover that the kind of energy you are getting from the fruit is electrical energy? You also obtain electrical energy from a dry cell battery. Just like a dry cell, the lemon has chemicals in it. Citrus fruits, like lemon, lime, tangerine, grapefruit, and orange, contain relatively high levels of acetic acid. This chemical reacted with the two dissimilar metals, the nail and copper wire, to produce electricity. Thus when you attached the wires to the antenna, you heard static (a spark-like) noise on the radio speaker. This was caused by the electrical energy being converted by the speaker into sound. If you have a voltmeter, you will be able to measure the energy generated by the fruit.

Make your own electric game.

Try the following Backyard Scientist project to discover the answer.

THE FOLLOWING PROJECT MUST BE DONE UNDER THE SUPERVISION OF AN ADULT.

Gather the following supplies:

One electric bicycle horn, batteries to fit the horn, a wood board about 1/4" x 4" x 12" , 1 piece of cardboard about 4" x 8", 1 roll of heavy duty aluminum foil, 8 thumb tacks, 2 wood screws (small and short so they don't go through the bottom of the wood when they are screwed in), some coins, and large and small paper clips. NOTE: You can use a buzzer, battery, and battery holder available at Radio Shack if you don't have a bicycle horn.

Start Experimenting:

1. Have an adult help you cut the wood board to about 4" by 12".
2. Have an adult help you cut the cardboard to 4" x 8" to fit onto the wood board.
3. Cut the center of the foil as the drawing shows. You must have a gap between the two pieces of foil.
4. Place the foil onto the cardboard, and press the thumb tacks through the foil to mount it on the cardboard. Do not completely push in the top tacks.
5. Mount the horn on top of the wood, using the small wood screws.
6. Cut the wires from the button switch of the horn. Insert these wires under the top of the thumb tacks on each strip of foil on the cardboard as you place the cardboard onto the wood. You may have to attach short pieces of wire to these if the wire from the horn is too short to reach the thumb tacks. You could put the foil directly onto the wood, but the cardboard is easy to replace, and this way you can make spare circuits to keep on hand if the foil tears from use.
7. Now put the batteries inside your horn.
8. Toss some coins or paper clips, one at a time, onto the board and observe what happens.

Can you answer the following questions from your observations?

1. What happened when you threw a coin or paper clip onto the board?
2. Did it matter where the paper clip or coin landed on the board?
3. Try tossing other objects onto the board and see what happens.
4. Does it make a difference what the object is made of that you throw onto the board?
5. Did you hear the horn go off? What do you think makes this happen?

Backyard Scientist solution to experiment.

When you throw metal objects such as coins, or paper clips, the metal completes the electric circuit between the strips of foil. The horn will sound when the electric circuit is complete. The circuit can only be completed with a conductive material such as metal. Glass, plastic, wood and other non-conductive materials will not complete the electric circuit. A circuit means a continuous flow of electricity to accomplish a purpose.

You can also replace the horn with a light bulb, socket, and battery holder mounted on the board instead of the horn. You can use both if you have them available. Use a lamp to match the voltage of the battery. Socket, lamp, battery holder and battery are available at Radio Shack Stores. Connect one wire from the battery holder to the lamp socket. Connect the other wire from the battery holder to one of the thumb tack contacts. Connect a wire from the other lamp connector to the other thumb tack contact on the other piece of foil.

What are the deep holes on the moon?

Try the following Backyard Scientist experiment to discover the answer.

Gather the following supplies:

One pencil, 1 sheet of paper 8-1/2" by 11", a ruler, 1 large bowl, 1 box of dry plaster of Paris, 1 large spoon, several balls or small objects of different weights and sizes, such as ping pong balls, rubber balls, pebbles, rocks, marbles, and 1 spray bottle filled with water.

BEFORE YOU BEGIN THE FOLLOWING EXPERIMENT, MAKE A CHART OF THE MOON. ADULT SUPERVISION IS REQUIRED ON THIS EXPERIMENT.

1. Have an adult help you make a chart with the ruler, pencil and sheet of paper. Make columns with the following headings: Date, Time, Shapes of Moon, and Location in the Sky. You can also record other observations about what you observe.
2. Find a good spot in your house where you can get a clear view of the sky each evening, or go outside accompanied by an adult.
3. With the help of an adult, observe the moon as often as you can for one month. On the chart, keep a record of what you observe each evening.
4. Before starting the next steps, you should go to the library and look at pictures of the moon.

Start Experimenting:

1. Fill the bottom of the bowl with enough of the dry plaster of Paris to fill it to a depth of at least two inches. This represents the moon's surface.
2. Take one of your balls and hold it about three feet over the bowl, then let it drop onto the dry plaster powder.
3. Examine the structure of the crater made by the impact of the ball.
4. Now experiment by dropping, from different heights, a few more of the items from the supplies you have gathered. Observe carefully what is taking place.
5. What is affecting the size and depth of the craters you are making on your moon?
6. Make several more impacts with the items you have until they begin to overlap and the old craters begin to get destroyed by the new ones.
7. Watch the surface of your plaster powder very carefully, and when it begins to look like the library pictures of the moon's surface, you have created a "lunar landscape."
8. When you are satisfied with your lunar landscape, gently spray the surface with a fine mist of water. Allow this to dry and you will have a surface that is hard and ready to display. If you wish you can now paint your model moon. Moon rocks are various shades of greys and browns.

Can you answer the following questions from your observations?

1. How did the items you dropped onto the structure of the crater change the appearance of your moon's surface?
2. Do you know what the deep holes on the moon seen by astronomers are called?

3. Does the moon have many craters that you can see when you look at it at night?
4. How do you think the craters on the moon were formed?
5. Do you know where the biggest crater on Earth is found?
6. Can you see many craters on Earth?

Backyard Scientist solution to experiment.

You saw that the surface of your moon got rougher as you dropped the items into it. The next time you have the opportunity, go to an observatory and look closely at the moon through a telescope or use a strong pair of binoculars at home. You will discover that you can see flat places and high ridges and low mountains. You will also see deep holes called craters. The craters on the moon were made by large chunks of rock (meteors) from space hitting the moon. These are called impact craters. The other type of crater found in nature is the volcanic crater formed by erupting volcanoes.

Some space material does hit the Earth. However, the Earth's surface has far fewer craters than the moon. Space material that reaches the Earth's atmosphere usually burns up from the heat caused by the friction of passing through the air, thus there are few impact craters on earth. Because of the Earth's weather, most traces of old crater impacts have disappeared. This is due to wind and water erosion. The largest crater in the United States is Meteor Crater near Winslow, Arizona.

To learn more about the moon and planets, go to the library. What is earth's nearest neighbor and where does the moon get its light? Which planets have more than one moon?

Do you think all sand contains magnetic material?

Try the following Backyard Scientist experiment to discover the answer.

THE FOLLOWING EXPERIMENT IS FUN TO DO WITH YOUR FAMILY, OR IN A CLASSROOM, OR WITH A WHOLE GROUP OF PEOPLE.

Gather the following supplies:

Lots of iron filings. If you don't have iron filings and the school supply store near you doesn't carry them, you can make your own, (see below for instructions), 1 cup naturally occurring sand (not the kind purchased for sand boxes), 1 small magnet, 1 bowl or flat paper plate, and one or more plastic lids from a coffee can (any size will do).

BEFORE YOU START THIS EXPERIMENT, IF THE SAND IN YOUR AREA DOES NOT CONTAIN IRON, ADD 3 TBSP. IRON FILINGS TO ONE CUP OF SAND.

If you cannot purchase iron filings in your area, you can make them a couple of different ways. Use steel wool, without soap in it (available in hardware and paint stores), and cut it into tiny bits with a pair of scissors. You can also use iron filings from a machine shop, or make your own by using a file and some material made with iron or steel.

Start Experimenting:

1. Pour a cup of sand into your bowl or paper plate.
2. Run your fingers through the sand. What do you find?
3. Take the magnet and hold it right above the surface of the sand. What are you observing? Can you see something being attracted to the magnet? Is something sticking to the magnet? If none of the above is happening, you will have to put the iron filings in the sand and try the above instructions again.
4. Feel the furriness or stickiness of the material sticking to the magnet. Take some off in your hand and feel its texture change.
5. Take the plastic lid and sprinkle some iron filings onto the plastic lid.
6. Hold a magnet under the lid. Observe what is happening.
7. Place some other materials on the lid, or add more plastic lids under the one containing the iron filings and observe. Keep adding thicknesses of material until nothing happens.

Can you answer the following questions from your observations?

1. Do you see the iron filings being pulled toward the magnet?
2. What do you think this is called?
3. When you put the magnet under the plastic lid with the iron filings in it, were you able to make some interesting patterns?
4. When you are all done experimenting, take the magnet and move it around the filings. Then scrape the filings from the magnet into their container. This makes it easier to return the iron filings to their container.

Backyard Scientist solution to experiment.

The fine black material you see in many naturally occurring sands is called magnetite. It is a form of iron ore. The stiffness of the material on the magnet is caused by the magnet's magnetic field. Not all sand has this fine black material in it.

The sand that sticks to the magnet is not magnetic. It is "glued" there by the magnetic material in the sand in combination with the magnetic field surrounding the magnet.

Small grains of magnetite are used by many creatures from bacteria to pigeons. Pigeons use magnetism to help them find their way home.

The space affected by a magnet is called a magnetic field. It is the area where the force of a magnet acts or can be felt. Iron filings can be used to see these lines of force. Did you make some interesting patterns when you put the magnet under the lid with the iron filings?

More magnet experiments may be found in "The Original Backyard Scientist."

Do you know what chalk is composed of?

Try the following Backyard Scientist experiment to discover the answer.

REMEMBER, ALWAYS HAVE AN ADULT WITH YOU WHEN YOU ARE EXPERIMENTING.

NEVER EAT OR DRINK ANYTHING YOU ARE EXPERIMENTING WITH UNLESS AN ADULT INSTRUCTS YOU TO DO SO.

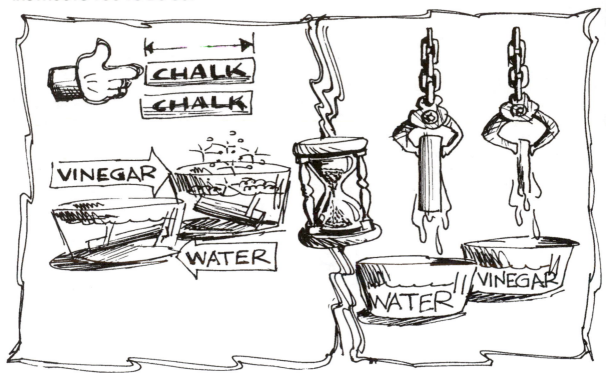

Gather the following supplies:

Two sticks of chalk exactly the same size, 2 small plastic bowls (the kind margarine comes in are fine), 1 small bottle of white distilled vinegar, water, 2 labels, 1 pencil or pen, a ruler, a piece of paper, and a table top to work on that water and vinegar will not damage.

Start Experimenting:

1. Mark one label "water" and the other label "vinegar".
2. With the ruler, measure the length of a piece of chalk and write its length on the label marked "vinegar".
3. Put the chalk into one of the bowls and attach the label to the outside of the bowl.
4. Measure the other piece of chalk and place it into the other bowl. Mark its length on the label marked "water." Attach the label to the outside of the second bowl.

5. Fill the bowl marked vinegar with vinegar and the bowl marked water with water.
6. Now watch the bowls for about 10 minutes. Observe very carefully what is taking place in each bowl. You might want to write down some notes on the piece of paper while you are watching the experiment.
7. Leave the chalk sticks untouched in their containers for about 20 minutes. After 20 minutes, take the chalk out of the vinegar solution and measure it with the ruler. Write down its length. Now wash your hands and take the chalk out of the water and measure its length with the ruler. Write down its length. Be sure to wash your hands after you have completed each measurement.
8. You may leave the chalk in the bowls overnight and make another observation in the morning. It would be fun to record the results.

Can you answer the following questions from your observations?

1. Are there any bubbles in the bowls?
2. Which bowl has the bubbles in it?
3. What did you discover when you measured the length of the chalk in each bowl?
4. Which piece is now shorter—the one that was in the vinegar or the one that was in the water?
5. Do you know what chalk is made of? If you do not know, take a guess.

Backyard Scientist solution to experiment.

The bubbles you see in the bowl containing the chalk and vinegar are bubbles of carbon dioxide gas (CO_2). The bubbles form on the surface of the chalk. Vinegar is a common acid. It is a mixture of acetic acid and water.

The bubbles will stop forming when all the acid has reacted with the chalk. The chalk in the vinegar gets smaller because the acetic acid breaks down the limestone in the chalk. No bubbles form in the bowl of water because water by itself will not react chemically with the chalk.

Chalk is made of a mineral called limestone. Another name for limestone is calcium carbonate. Limestone is also used to make cement. Limestone has also been used for many years to make statues. When acid gets on limestone, the calcium carbonate is broken down. Calcium ions and carbon dioxide gas are two chemicals that are formed in this chemical reaction.

For further experimenting with chalk, cut some chalk into short lengths. Using small plastic bowls, test other solutions on the chalk and record your results on a piece of paper. For instance, you might want to try various types of juice like orange, lemon, apple, cranberry, punch, or any other kind you might have around. Measure each piece of chalk carefully before the liquids come into contact with the chalk and then measure again in 20 or 30 minutes. Record your observations, and write down the name of the other liquids you are using on a label attached to each bowl. Discard the juices after each test.

A concern our country faces is acid rain formed when chemicals resulting from the burning of coal and other fossil fuels come into contact with rain. The sulfur in the air, produced by burning coal and oil, combines with the moisture in the atmosphere to form sulfuric acid which falls to the earth as rain. This can kill vegetation, pollute waterways and damage bridges and other structures. This experiment demonstrated how powerful even a relatively weak acid like acetic acid is and its affects on materials.

Exploring density. What will float or sink?

Try the following Backyard Scientist experiment to discover the answer.

THIS EXPERIMENT MUST BE DONE UNDER THE SUPERVISION OF AN ADULT.

Gather the following supplies:

Two 8-10 oz. clear plastic cups (size is not that important), 1 cup salt, 16 oz. water, 5 oz. rubbing alcohol, food coloring, 1 rubber band, a dry bean, a popcorn kernel, a piece of Styrofoam, a grape or raisin, a penny, a small ball of aluminum foil, and paper and pencil.

Start Experimenting:

1. First make a saturated solution of salt water by pouring about 8 oz. of water into one of the cups and adding salt until no more will dissolve in the water. Stir constantly while adding the salt.
2. Pour some of the saturated salt water solution into the other cup. You will want the salt water to be about two inches deep.
3. Add a drop or two of food coloring to the remaining plain water and carefully pour until there is another two inches of water in the cup on top of the saturated water. Do this by tipping the receiving cup to its side until the water almost comes out the top. Pour the water down the inside surface of the cup. You want the two layers to remain as separate as possible. Some minor mixing will occur.
4. Now do the same with the rubbing alcohol. If you want to, you may add a different color of food coloring to the rubbing alcohol.
5. Draw three columns on the paper. Title the first column "Articles." List the articles you will drop into the glass containing the three liquids. Title the second column "Predictions" and the third column "Observations."
6. The next step is to carefully begin dropping the remaining articles into the cup containing the three liquids. Before dropping the objects, you should predict how far each object will sink.

Can you answer the following questions from your observations?

1. Did you notice the liquids floated on top of each other?
2. Which liquid had the highest density and which the lowest density?
3. By dropping the objects into the cup with the three liquids, what did you observe about the objects and the liquids?

Backyard Scientist solution to experiment.

The cup contained three liquids, each of a different density. The objects you dropped into the cup also had different densities. Objects floated on the liquid that was more dense than the objects. They sank through liquids that were of lower density than the objects. Some of the objects were denser than any of the three liquids in the cup. Water is one of the most dense liquids. Adding salt makes it even denser. Is ocean water denser than fresh drinking water? Can you float better in ocean water than in fresh water? Ocean water contains dissolved salt and other minerals. It is denser than fresh water. The denser a liquid is, the more easily objects float on it. Generally, the more easily a liquid evaporates the less dense the liquid. Alcohol evaporates more rapidly than water, so it is less dense than water. Density is defined as the mass of a substance per unit of volume.

Suggestions for further experimenting.

Try layering different liquids. Drop other small objects into the cups. Try changing the temperatures of the liquids by cooling them or heating them. Temperature affects density.

Does it stick or doesn't it? Exploring Molecular Cohesion and Surface Tension.

Try the following Backyard Scientist experiment to discover the answer.

Gather the following supplies:

Four small plastic cups (any size), food coloring, 2 oz. water, 1 oz. rubbing alcohol, 1 oz. cooking oil, 1/2 oz. liquid dish detergent, several swizzle sticks or drinking straws, a piece of wax paper or a pie tin to experiment on and several toothpicks.

SPECIAL NOTE: 2 tbsp. = 1 oz., 1 tbsp. = 1/2 oz., 1 tbsp. = 3 tsp.

Start Experimenting:

1. Pour half the water into a cup and add a drop of food coloring.
2. Use the straw or swizzle stick to transfer the liquid from the cup. Place several drops of the colored water onto the wax paper or pie pan/baking dish. You do this by putting the straw into the liquid, then place your finger over the other end. Release your finger when you are ready to place the drop onto the surface.
3. Try to dissect (cut) one of the drops in half using a toothpick. Observe what happens.
4. Push two drops of water very close to each other, but not touching. Observe what happens.
5. With an unused swizzle stick or straw, add a drop of alcohol to a drop of water. Observe what happens.
6. Again using an unused swizzle stick or straw, add a drop of cooking oil to another drop of water. Observe what happens. Use a clean toothpick to try to mix the two together. Can you do it?
7. Dip one of the toothpicks into the liquid dish detergent and touch it to another drop of water. Observe what happens.
8. To the drop of water with the oil surrounding it, add a drop of liquid detergent. Observe what takes place.

Can you answer the following questions from your observations?

1. What happened to the two drops of water when they were pushed very close to one another?
2. Were you able to cut the water drop in half with the toothpick?
3. Did the water and oil mix together? What happened when you added the detergent?
4. What happened when you added the detergent to the drop of water? Why did this take place?

Backyard Scientist solution to experiment.

Molecules of the same kind attract each other with a very strong, equal force in all directions. The perfect and strongest naturally occurring shape in nature is the sphere. Liquids will mix with each other when their surface tension or cohesiveness is destroyed. The chemicals in the liquid detergent broke down the surface tension of the water and oil. One end of the long molecule in the detergent is very much attracted to water, the other is very much attracted to oil, so it attaches itself to both of these molecules allowing them to mix.

The two drops of water, when pushed near each other, seemed to gobble each other up because water molecules have strong affinity for each other. When you added oil to the water, the molecules did not combine, because the molecules do not have an affinity for one another. When you added detergent to the water drop, the drop flattened out. That is because the surface tension of the water was destroyed. The detergent also allowed the oil and water molecules to mix, using the detergent molecules as facilitators. The alcohol and water really did not mix. After a few seconds the alcohol just evaporated away. Its molecules have very low cohesion. Again, because water molecules have a great affinity for one another and water is very flexible, it was very hard to cut the drop of water in half with the toothpick.

Do you know how to make an electric buzzer?

Try the following Backyard Scientist project to discover the answer.

YOU WILL NEED THE HELP OF AN ADULT FOR THIS EXCITING PROJECT.

Gather the following supplies:

A wood base about 3/4" x 4" x 4", three 1" 90 degree angle brackets, 1 single-pole single-throw switch, a 4" bolt 10/24 or larger, 2 nuts for the bolt, five #8 x 1/2" wood or sheet metal screws, one 1" x 8/32 screw with 3 nuts for the contactor, enough insulated bell wire for at least 200 turns (about 20 feet of wire), 1 hacksaw blade for the vibrator (this must be cleaned at contact point), small piece of sandpaper and one 6 volt lantern battery. You will also need a screwdriver and pliers for assembly.

Start Experimenting:

1. First study the diagram and read all the instructions.
2. Lay out the three brackets on the wood base and mount the angle brackets and screws per the drawing. Mount the switch.
3. Install the contact points. Then mount vibrator (hacksaw blade) on the correct bracket. Bend and break the blade just past the contact point.
4. Cut two 8" leads from the wire, then wrap the remaining bell wire around the 4" bolt in tight coils. Always wind in the same direction. Leave 5" of wire at the beginning and end of the coil you are winding. This is your electro magnet or field coil. Install the coil onto its bracket and tighten with a nut.
5. Now you are ready to make your hook up.
6. Take one end of the wire coil and connect it to the contact bracket. Connect the other wire to the switch. Take the 8" wire leads and attach one to the armature (vibrator) bracket, and the other to the switch.
7. Connect these wires to the battery, and the buzzer will work when the switch is in the closed position and if the contact screw is properly adjusted.
8. Adjust the contact screw so the vibrating blade just touches the end of the screw. Adjust the field coil bolt untill it is very close to the vibrator, but not touching.

Can you answer the following questions from your observations?

1. How did you make electricity work?
2. Can you draw the buzzer you just made on a piece of paper and trace the flow of the electricity to see why the buzzer sounds?
3. What can you compare the coil to?
4. Did you notice the small spark at the tip of the vibrator as it opened and closed?

Backyard Scientist solution to experiment.

Electricity flows from the battery through the switch (if used) to the coil wound on the bolt, and then to the contact. When the circuit is complete, through the vibrator, the coil becomes an electro magnet pulling the blade to the coil and breaking the circuit. The blade will then return to the contact completing the circuit. This will start the action over again. As the circuit is closed and broken (acting like a switch), a buzzing noise is heard. This principle also applies to an electric motor. There are many types of electrical motors, some very large, some very small. It would be interesting to do research on their history and the different types that are available.

Do you know what viscosity is?

Try the following Backyard Scientist experiment to discover the answer.

ADULT SUPERVISION IS REQUIRED ON THIS EXPERIMENT.

Gather the following supplies:

Three pieces of 1" diameter (smaller or larger dia. is OK), clear rigid plastic tubing about 3 feet long—each must be of the same length (please see end of experiment for where to get the plastic tubes); 6 caps to tightly fit the plastic tubes, food coloring, ordinary cooking oil, 20 or 30 weight motor oil, a roll of clear packaging tape, duct tape, water; or 3 tall narrow jars, all the same size with lids, can be substituted for the three tubes if you cannot obtain them.

Start Experimenting:

1. Seal one end of each tube with pipe caps using the duct tape.
2. Fill one tube with water (add a little food coloring to liven up the appearance). Be sure to leave space for a little air, so an air bubble can move up through the liquid. Seal the other end of the tube the same as before.

3. Fill the second tube with ordinary cooking oil. Leave the same amount of space for air as in the first tube. Seal the other end of the tube as you did in instruction number 2.
4. Fill the third tube with 20 or 30 weight motor oil. Again, leave the same amount of space for air. Seal the other end of the tube as you did in instruction number 2.

5. Stand the tubes on end, so they are even, and tape the three tubes together with clear plastic tape.
6. Leave the tubes standing on their end for a minute. Now turn the tubes onto their other end for a minute. Then turn them over again.
7. Compare the different rates of speed the air bubbles move up through the different liquids.
8. Do this a couple of times, and think about the liquids and the air bubbles racing in them.

Can you answer the following questions from your observations?

1. Do you know what viscosity means?
2. What did you observe when you turned over the three tubes of liquids?
3. In which liquid did the air bubble travel fastest and slowest? Which bubble came in second?
4. Which one of the three liquids do you think would make the best lubricant and why?
5. If a lubricant is too viscous, what effect could this have on the parts of a very complex piece of equipment?
6. What could happen to a very expensive machine if a lubricant is not viscous enough?
7. Why do you think it is important for modern technology to know which lubricants are best?

Backyard Scientist solution to experiment.

Viscosity is a characteristic of all liquids. Not all liquids make good lubricants, even if they are viscous. For example, honey is very viscous, but it does not make a good lubricant. Liquids that oxidize (combine with oxygen) such as vegetable oils make poor lubricants. The more viscous a liquid is, the more resistance it offers to any change in form.

The viscosity of a liquid is a measure of its thickness and its resistance to flow. A lubricant's viscosity is an important factor in deciding whether it should be used for a particular purpose.

Based on viscosity alone, the motor oil makes the best lubricant, the cooking oil the next best, and the water the least best lubricant. This is because the motor oil is the most viscous. The bubble took longer to move up the column of motor oil. The bubble in the cooking oil reached the top of the tube second after the water. That means the cooking oil was more viscous than the water, but less viscous than the motor oil. The water was the least viscous of the three liquids.

If a lubricant is too viscous, it can clog or slow down moving parts. If a liquid is not viscous enough, it can cause machine parts to heat up and wear out. This could be very costly for a company. Lubricants are extremely important in modern technology. The right amount of the right lubricant, in the right place, at the right time, will allow cars, airplanes, boats, electrical generators and almost all industrial equipment to run smoothly. Without lubricants, today's forms of transportation and production would grind to a halt. Other factors are also considered by engineers. These factors include the lubricant's ability to withstand heat, their non-corrosiveness, their ability not to absorb other chemicals, and their ability not to break down under adverse conditions.

The clear rigid tubing may be obtained from local tubing or plastic companies or Ryan Herco, P. O. Box 588, Burbank, CA 91503. They have a number of locations in the country. They have a catalog from which you can order.

Now turn the page for an exciting experiment on how to measure viscosity.

How would you measure viscosity?

Try the following Backyard Scientist experiment to discover the answer.

ADULT SUPERVISION IS REQUIRED ON THIS EXPERIMENT. PLEASE COMPLETE THE PREVIOUS EXPERIMENT ON VISCOSITY BEFORE DOING THIS EXPERIMENT.

Before starting this experiment, you will have to make a chart (see sample drawing). Set yours up the same way.

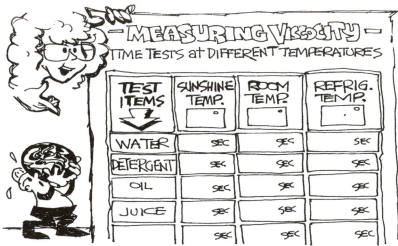

Gather the following supplies:

Three or more clear plastic tubes 1" to 2" diameter and of equal length (about 12 inches long), the same kind you used in the previous experiment with only the bottoms capped (you can substitute 3 or more narrow jars, all the same size); several marbles or ball bearings of the same size; water, food coloring, motor oil, different kinds of clear juices, cooking oils, clear shampoos, clear soap detergents; 1 measuring cup, 3 plastic cups for each liquid you are measuring, a watch with a second hand, paper towels, and pencil and paper for marking the tubes/jars. It is much easier to do the experiment if you have a tube for each liquid you are measuring. If you reuse the tubes, thoroughly wash them before putting another liquid into it. This will insure more accurate results.

Start Experimenting:

1. If you are going to use the narrow plastic tubes from the previous experiment, have an adult help you cut the clear plastic tubes to about 12 inches long. You can use narrow jars as an alternative as previously suggested.
2. Sort all the liquids you have collected into groups (oil, motor oil, soap/detergent, shampoos, juices and etc.).

3. Fill one tube with water, then pour this into a measuring glass to measure the volume of liquid the tube will hold.
4. Now pour this same amount from each liquid you will use into plastic cups. Be sure to mark the cups with the type of liquid that is in it.
5. Place these plastic cups into the refrigerator. Keep them in the refrigerator for a few hours, or overnight, until the liquids are very cold.

6. Do the same thing again as in instruction number 4, only this time put the plastic cups full of the different liquids directly into the sun for a few hours, or all day, until the liquids feel warm.
7. Repeat the same procedure again as in instruction number 4. This time you can start the experiment, because you want these liquids at room temperature.
8. Take your tubes, or jars, and fill them with the different kinds of liquids. Label each tube or jar with the name of the liquid in it.
9. Get your clock or watch ready.
10. Drop a marble into your first liquid, and measure how long it takes for the marble to reach the bottom. Mark the results on your chart. Continue the process with all the liquids you wish to test. If you use the marbles over again, be sure to clean them well before dropping them into the next liquid.
11. Now test all the refrigerated liquids using the same procedure as in instruction number 10.
12. Now test all the liquids warmed in the sun using the same procedure as in instruction number 10.

Can you answer the following questions from your observations?

1. Which liquid was the most viscous?
2. Did you notice a difference in viscosity in the same liquids when cooled in the refrigerator, or at room temperature?
3. What happened to the liquid's viscosity when warmed by the sun? What differences did you observe?
4. Did any of the liquids you used become more viscous when heated?
5. Can solids become viscous liquids?
6. How do you think you could measure viscosity accurately?

Backyard Scientist solution to experiment.

As the temperature of liquids rise, their viscosity decreases. As the temperature of the liquids decreases, they become more viscous. Here are some examples of the viscosity of various liquids at 20 degrees Celsius.

water - 1.0050, ethyl alcohol - 1.192, olive oil - 80.8, lubricating oil - 92.0.

As you can see, the higher the viscosity of the liquid, the better lubricant that liquid could be. Remember all viscous liquids do not make good lubricants. Liquids that readily combine with oxygen (oxidize) do not make good lubricants.
There are several formulas for measuring viscosity. These can be found in the encyclopedia.

Solids can become viscous liquids. For example, when paraffin wax is heated, the wax will become a viscous liquid. Metals, when melted, become viscous liquids. As their temperatures are raised, they become less viscous. Did you know that our bodies produce one of the most wondrous lubricants in the world? It is called Synovial Fluid and lubricates your joints such as elbows, knees and hips. You might want to go to the library and research lubricants in your body. You will find it very interesting. It would be fun to write a research paper on this subject.

Exploring Turbidity.

Try the following Backyard Scientist experiment to discover the answer.

ADULT SUPERVISION IS REQUIRED ON THIS EXPERIMENT.

Gather the following supplies:

One 3 to 4 inch diameter rigid clear plastic PVC tubing 4 or 5 feet long (a source is listed at the end of experiment), 2 pipe caps to fit the pipe, PVC cement, coarse sand (like construction sand), food coloring, clock or watch with a second hand, a strainer and duct tape.

REMEMBER, ALWAYS HAVE AN ADULT WITH YOU WHEN YOU ARE EXPERIMENTING.

NEVER EAT OR DRINK ANYTHING YOU ARE EXPERIMENTING WITH UNLESS AN ADULT INSTRUCTS YOU TO DO SO.

Start Experimenting:

1. Cement a cap to one end of the pipe.
2. Using the strainer, sift the construction sand. Discard the fine sand and retain the coarser material for the experiment.
3. Fill the pipe with water and add a little food coloring (not too much or the water will become too dark to see through).
4. Measure one cup, or more, of the coarse remnants of sand and put into the pipe.
5. Put the other end cap on and hold it in place with duct tape. Make sure you seal it very well. The tape will allow you to easily remove one end to drain out the water. The tube is now very heavy with the water in it.
6. Have an adult help you turn the tube over so that it stands on one end, and observe. After letting the sand settle, turn the tube over to about a 45 degree angle and observe very carefully what is happening. Repeat the procedure, and time the event with the watch or clock.
7. Stand the tube on one end again, letting the sand settle.
8. Turn the tube over 180 degrees rapidly to stand it on its other end. Observe what happens. Repeat this procedure and time how long it takes the sand to travel to the other end.

Can you answer the following questions from your observations?

1. What would happen if you didn't sift out the fine sand?
2. When you turned the tube over on its end, what did you observe about the sand?
3. When you turned the tube to about a 45 degree angle, what did you notice the sand doing this time?

4. With what do you think you can compare the moving mass of sand?
5. What affected the moving sand mass?
6. When did the sand move down the tube fastest—when the tube was turned 45 degrees or 180 degrees?

Backyard Scientist solution to experiment.

The device you have just made is called a Turbidity Column. If you didn't sift out all the fine sand, you would have a lot of mud inside the tube. When you turned the column over on its end, you saw the particles of sand move down to the other end in a random fashion. When you turned the tube at about a 45 degree angle, you saw the sand particles move in a group. You also saw the difference in the speed the sand traveled down the tube. It traveled much faster when the tube was at a 45 degree angle than it did at the 180 degree angle. Some researchers think that the moving mass of sand at the 45 degree angle simulates the effects of an airplane wing, and that the water beneath the mass of moving sand and the inside wall of the tube is at a higher pressure than the water flowing over the moving sand. This is the same principle that keeps an airplane in flight. When you turned the turbidity tube on its end, the sand had to move through the resistance of the water molecules. The sand actually collided with these molecules. The sand mass was also affected by the liquid's viscosity which we learned about in previous experiments.

You can order the tube for this experiment from the same company that supplies the rigid tubing for the viscosity experiments.

What do you know about buoyancy?

Try the following Backyard Scientist experiment to discover the answer.

NOTE:
THIS EXPERIMENT IS REALLY GREAT TO DO WITH YOUR FAMILY, OR A GROUP OF PEOPLE, AND IS ALSO GOOD FOR BIRTHDAY PARTIES.

Gather the following supplies:

At least two (more are better) 8" or 9" balloons, any tall see-through wide mouth container about 2 or 3 gallon capacity, a funnel, one 3 or 4 oz. plastic or paper cup, about 2 cups of sand (any kind), a plastic spoon, pencil and paper to write on, access to water, and a table top to work on that won't be damaged when it gets wet.

Start Experimenting:

1. Fill the cup with sand.
2. Place the small end of the funnel into the neck of a balloon. Measure two spoonfuls of sand from your small cup and put them into the balloon.
3. Tie the opening of the balloon containing the sand.
4. Take another balloon and repeat step number 2.
5. Blow a little air into the balloon. Tie the balloon opening.
6. Now take the container and fill it within an inch or two from the top with water.
7. Drop the first balloon into the container of water. Observe what has happened to the first balloon. Using the pencil and paper, record your first observation.
8. Now repeat step number 7 with the second balloon. Observe and record your observation.
9. Fill the remaining balloons with different amounts of sand and air. Keep track of the amount of sand and number of puffs of air in each balloon. Record this information and the results of placing the balloons in the water on your chart.

Can you answer the following questions from your observations?

1. Did the balloon with just the sand (no air) in it float or sink?
2. Did the balloon with the sand and air in it float or sink?
3. When you were experimenting with different amounts of air and sand, did the balloons float at different levels in the container of water?
4. What factors do you think determine the way the balloon will float in the water—the amount of air, the amount of sand, or the amount of both in the balloon?

5. Do you think you can get a balloon to float exactly halfway between the surface and the bottom of the container? How would you do it? This is really fun to try to do.

Backyard Scientist solution to experiment.

Did you discover the balloon containing only the sand sank rapidly to the bottom of the container? The balloon with some air in it floated somewhere between the top of the water and the bottom. Did you notice when you experimented with different amounts of sand and air, the balloons floated at different levels depending on the amount of each they contained? A real challenge will be to get a balloon to float exactly halfway between the surface and the bottom. You can do this by either varying the amount of sand in the balloon, or the amount of air in the balloon. From this experiment we learn that objects more dense than water will sink and objects less dense will float. Density is the quantity per unit of volume, or another way to express it is the mass of a substance per unit volume. This is expressed in grams per cubic centimeter or ounces per cubic inch.

To add another factor to the density equation, change the temperature of the water in the container by adding ice cubes or adding hot water. Number the balloons so you can compare the levels at which they float in different water temperatures.

If you happen to have a bar of Ivory Soap around, try putting this in the container of water and observe what happens. Now take another bar of soap (different brand), and put it into the water and observe what happens.

Can you measure the effects of evaporation?

Try the following Backyard Scientist experiment to discover the answer.

Gather the following supplies:

Two 24 or 32 oz. plastic or paper cups, 2 small paper plates, 2 small paper cups (about 4 oz.), 1 plastic straw, 1 straight pin, rubbing alcohol, water, ruler, scissors, several strips of paper towel cut about 1" wide x 8" long, rubber gloves, and an adult to help you.

CAUTION: RUBBING ALCOHOL IS POISONOUS AND FLAMMABLE. HAVE AN ADULT HELP YOU WITH THE ALCOHOL AND NEVER EAT OR DRINK ANYTHING YOU ARE EXPERIMENTING WITH UNLESS INSTRUCTED TO DO SO IN THE EXPERIMENT. ALWAYS WASH YOUR HANDS AFTER EVERY EXPERIMENT.

Start Experimenting:

1. Place the two large cups, side-by-side, near a window or in a warm place.
2. Using the ruler, measure the length of the straw and find its center.
3. Insert the pin through the exact center of the straw, allowing equal amounts of the pin to protrude from each side.
4. Put the straw between the cups with the pin resting on the rim of each cup. You have just made a balance scale.
5. Put on the rubber gloves. Pour water into one of the small paper cups and fill the other with rubbing alcohol.
6. Still wearing the gloves, place a strip of paper towel on a plate and pour water on it, wetting it evenly. Drain any excess liquid back into the cup containing the water.
7. Wet another strip of towel, this time using the alcohol. Drain the excess back into the cup containing the alcohol.
8. Hang the strip wetted with water on one end of the straw and the strip wetted with alcohol on the other end of the straw.
9. You may have to adjust the balance of the straw so the strips hang about even. This is done by moving the strips along the length of the straw until the straw is horizontal.
10. Wash your hands with soap and warm water. Then return to your experiment.
11. Observe what happens to the strips of paper and the balance over the next 15 or 20 minutes.

Can you answer the following questions from your observations?

1. Which strip of paper dried the fastest?
2. What happened to the balance as the strips of paper dried?
3. Do you think all liquids evaporate at the same rate?

Backyard Scientist solution to experiment.

Did you discover that the strip soaked in alcohol dried more quickly than the strip soaked in water? The attraction, or cohesion, between molecules of alcohol is less than that of water molecules for each other. Alcohol molecules can break away from one another more easily and therefore evaporate more quickly than water molecules can. Try this same experiment using other liquids you have around the house. See which liquids have molecules with low or high cohesion.

Can plants find light?

Try the following Backyard Scientist experiment to discover the answer.

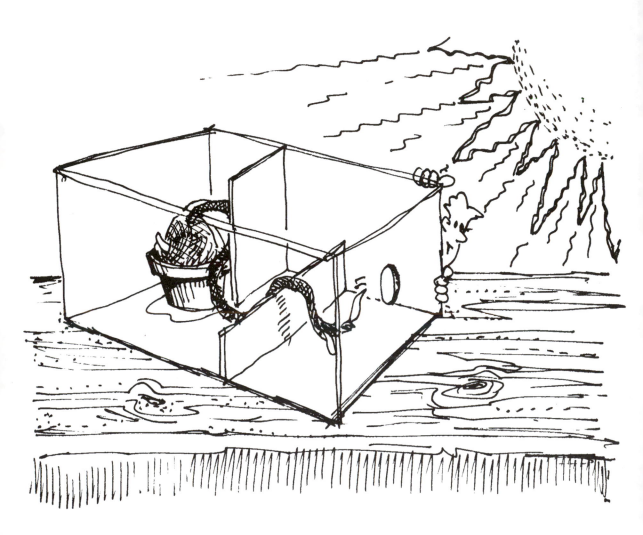

Gather the following supplies:

A potato that has begun sprouting, a pot large enough to hold the potato and some soil, a piece of stiff cardboard (like the flap of a corrugated box), masking tape, scissors, a medium size box that can be made light proof. This box must be several inches deeper than the pot is tall and 3 times longer than it is wide.

Start Experimenting:

1. Put some soil in the pot. Plant the potato in the soil. Add additional soil to almost fill the pot. Be sure the sprouting portion of the potato is above the soil.
2. Water the potato.
3. Make a wall inside the box about 1/3 of the distance from one end. Leave about 1/4 of the wall open at one side. Use the tape to attach the wall to the bottom and side of the box.
4. Cut a 2 inch diameter hole in one end of the box.
5. Put the potato in the box behind the wall. It should be at the end furthest away from the hole.
6. Close the lid tightly. You can use masking tape to seal the edges of the lid. You want only a single point where light can get into the box. This will be from the 2 inch hole you cut in one end of the box.
7. Every few days, take the box into a dimly lit area and unseal it. Give the potato a little water. Don't over water. If you do, the potato will rot and the experiment will end. Each time you open the box, observe the sprout of the potato.
8. Now plant a sprouting potato in the garden, or in a pot that you can place in a window. Water it regularly.

Can you answer the following questions from your observations?

1. In which direction did the sprout grow?
2. How long did it take for the sprout to grow towards the light?
3. What color was the sprout in the box?
4. What color was the sprout in the garden or inside the house near the window?
5. Why do you think the sprout in the box was so pale?
6. Which potato grew the fastest?

Backyard Scientist solution to experiment.

The sprout in the box grew towards the source of the light, the hole at the end of the box. Plants naturally grow in the direction of light. The sprout in the box was either white or a very pale green. The sprout that grew in the garden, or in the pot near the window, was a deep green color. That is because it had enough sunlight to make chlorophyll, the substance that gives plants and grass their green color. The plant inside the box did not have enough light to do that. While both potatoes received regular water and were planted at the same time, only the potato that received abundant light grew fast—the potato in the garden or near the window. To grow well, living things need enough water, air, light, and food. If people do not get enough light, they begin to look pale and not well. They will eventually become quite ill.

Can you "take a picture" without a camera or film?

Try the following Backyard Scientist experiment to discover the answer.

THE FOLLOWING EXPERIMENT IS FUN TO DO WITH YOUR FAMILY, GROUP, CLASS OR FRIENDS. ADULT SUPERVISION IS REQUIRED ON THIS EXPERIMENT.

Gather the following supplies:

An 8" x 10" piece of blueprint paper (see end of experiment on where to obtain). Keep the paper wrapped and away from light until you are ready to use it. You will also need 3% solution hydrogen peroxide (available at drug stores), 2 dishpans or aluminum foil trays at least 1/2" deep, paper towels, a tablespoon, 2 cups water, a box large enough to hold the blueprint paper, a piece of cardboard slightly larger than the blueprint paper, a room that can be darkened by pulling drapes or shades, and a sunny day. You will also need different objects with interesting shapes, such as cotton balls, Q-tips, rubber bands, tools, and jewelry. Also, natural objects like seashells, flowers, and weeds.

Start Experimenting:

1. Have an adult help you mix one tablespoon of hydrogen peroxide with one cup of fresh water in the dishpan or foil pan. Fill the other dishpan or foil tray with plain water.
2. Be sure to keep the blueprint paper wrapped until it is time to use it.
3. Take a piece of blueprint paper to a darkened room. Put the blueprint paper on the cardboard with the blue side facing up.
4. Take the objects you have collected and carefully arrange them on the blueprint paper (take your time). Create an interesting design with the objects you have.
5. After you have completed your design, carefully take the cardboard and your blueprint paper, with the objects on it, into the sunshine. Let the sun shine directly on it for two or three minutes, depending on how bright the sun is. Bring the empty box outside and put it next to your design.
6. After two or three minutes, remove the objects from your blueprint paper and put them into the empty box. Then carry the paper, holding it by its edges, quickly to the dishpan or foil pan that you have prepared with the water and hydrogen peroxide. You must always handle the blueprint paper by its edges so you do not smear the picture.
7. Now carefully slide the blueprint paper into the solution. Move the paper around in the solution for a few seconds. Observe very carefully what is happening to the blueprint paper. What changes are taking place?
8. When your design has turned light blue (this process takes a few minutes) remove the blueprint paper from the solution. Rinse your print in the tray of water. Blot it dry with a paper towel.
9. Set the damp print indoors on paper towels until it dries. You can now frame your print or show it to your friends.
10. You can make as many prints as you wish.

Can you answer the following questions from your observations?

1. When you mixed the peroxide and water in the pan what did you make?
2. When you put the print into the solution, what changes did you observe in the blueprint paper?
3. What kind of print did you make?
4. Why do you think you have to keep the blueprint paper wrapped until it is time to use?
5. Why do you have to arrange your print in a darkened room?

Backyard Scientist solution to experiment.

You have just made a "Photogram"! This is a shadow-like photograph made by putting objects between light sensitive paper and a light source. Where light hits the paper, it darkens slightly. Where light doesn't reach the paper (underneath the objects you've arranged on top) it remains unchanged. After the design is formed, the fixing solution, which you made with water and hydrogen peroxide, makes the picture permanent.

You can make very interesting patterns in your photograms. Use your imagination. There are many objects in your kitchen, your house, and your yard that will make unusual designs. It is often fun to make up photograms and have your family and friends guess what is in the picture.

You can order blueprint paper from many catalogs that carry science products. If you are having trouble finding it, you can write to me for sources. Blueprint paper usually comes in packages of 24 sheets and cost about $6.00 or $7.00.

Do you know for certain the shape of a snowflake?

Try the following Backyard Scientist experiment to discover the answer.

Gather the following supplies:

Make sure it is snowing outside. You will need, in addition to fresh snow, the following: 1 magnifying glass, 1 piece of black construction paper 8-1/2" by 11" or larger, 1 white dinner size paper plate and some clear plastic tape. If you live in a place where it does not snow then save this experiment until you visit someone where there is fresh snow.

BE SURE TO OBTAIN PERMISSION FROM AN ADULT TO GO OUTSIDE AND DO THIS EXPERIMENT.

Start Experimenting:

1. Before you go outside, take the piece of black construction paper and tape it flat to the white dinner plate.

2. Go outside while it is snowing. Be sure to wear warm clothing and gloves to protect you from the cold.

3. Catch some of the snowflakes onto the black paper.
4. Now examine the snowflakes very carefully with your magnifying glass. Be very careful not to steam up the magnifying glass or breathe too heavily on the snow flakes.
5. Repeat the above process a few times by having a variety of snowflakes to examine.
6. Now try making a snowball. Is this easy or difficult to do?
7. Place some clean snow and some dirty snow on the black paper and observe which one melts faster.

Can you answer the following questions from your observations?

1. What do the snowflakes look like?
2. How many sides or spokes do the snowflakes have?
3. Do all snowflakes look the same?
4. What is the one common characteristic of all snowflakes?
5. Which melts faster, clean snow or dirty snow?
6. Is it easier to make a snowball on a very cold day or when it is a little warmer? Why?
7. What do snowflakes turn into?
8. Do you know what happens when liquid water freezes?
9. Does ice protect living things in lakes and rivers?
10. Do you know why it sometimes snows? What causes a blizzard?

Backyard Scientist solution to experiment.

Did you discover that snowflakes have six sides or six spokes, and many snowflakes have branches like a tree? Each snowflake is different from every other one. Snow is formed instead of rain when water vapor very high in the atmosphere, in very cold air, freezes and turns into ice crystals instead of falling as water drops (rain).

The snow clouds are then filled with millions of snowflakes, just as rain clouds are filled with raindrops. The ice crystals get larger and heavier, and the snowflakes begin falling to earth from the effects of gravity. If the air at lower altitudes is warm enough, the ice crystals melt and become raindrops. When snowflakes get warm, they melt into drops of water. If the air is not warm enough, the ice crystals do not melt and fall to the ground as snow.

When liquid water freezes, it becomes a solid called ice. Ice protects living things in frozen lakes and rivers.

When fierce winds and very cold temperatures come along with the snow, the storm is called a blizzard. Sometimes, if there is little water vapor in the air, wind and cold make a blizzard without snowfall. The wind picks up "old" snow from the ground and blows it so hard it seems to come from the sky. Blizzards can be very dangerous, and it is best not to be out in one.

When we make snowballs, we compress the snow with our hands and this causes a slight melting of the ice crystals. When pressure is removed, refreezing occurs and binds the snow together. Making snowballs is difficult in very cold weather because the pressure we can apply is not great enough to melt the snow. An ice skater skates on a thin film of water between the blade and the ice, which is produced by blade pressure and friction. As soon as the pressure is released, the water refreezes.

Clean snow is a good reflector and therefore does not melt rapidly in sunlight. If the snow is dirty, it absorbs radiant energy from the sun and melts faster. Dropping black soot by aircraft on snowed in mountain sides is a technique sometimes used in flood control. Controlled melting, at favorable times, rather than a sudden runoff of melted snow is thereby accomplished.

Studying miscible and immiscible liquids.

Try the following Backyard Scientist experiment to discover the answer.

CAUTION: NEVER EAT OR DRINK ANYTHING YOU ARE EXPERIMENTING WITH. ADULT SUPERVISION IS NEEDED FOR THIS EXPERIMENT.

Gather the following supplies:

One bottle of cooking oil, access to water, green and blue food coloring, 1 bottle of rubbing alcohol, measuring cups, 1 large plastic bottle about 50 oz. with cap (mineral water bottles are great), a smaller one can be used, 1 tall, slender bottle or plastic test tube (an olive jar works well for this), and a marking pen or crayon. Remember to always cover your table top in case of spills.

Start Experimenting:

1. Fill the large bottle half full of tap water.
2. Add a few drops of blue food coloring to the water.
3. Measure one cup of oil and pour it into the bottle. The oil will float on the top of the water.
4. Screw the cap on tight.
5. Lay the bottle on its side and rock it back and forth (gently). This makes an ocean wave effect.
6. Shake the bottle and see if you can mix the water and oil together. Observe what is happening after you stop shaking the bottle.

7. Take the slender bottle and measure the length of the container with a ruler, then divide this length into thirds. Mark the three sections on the outside with a marking pen or crayon dividing the bottle or jar into three sections. Fill the jar to the first mark with water. Then add a few drops of food coloring.
8. Carefully pour in cooking oil, tilting the bottle or jar as you pour, filling the bottle to the second mark. Try not to mix the liquids. If they do mix, just let them stand for a minute and they will separate.
9. Gently pour in the alcohol to the third mark. After the alcohol is poured, color the alcohol with food coloring. Use a different color than you used to color the water.
10. Now cap the jar and carefully observe the contents that you just poured in.
11. Think about how you might get the alcohol to trade places with the water.
12. After you are finished making the water and alcohol trade places, vigorously shake the container.

Can you answer the following questions from your observations?

1. Can you get the oil and water to mix?
2. What is the scientific term for two liquids that will not mix together?
3. When you gave the bottle a hard shake what happened to the oil in the water?
4. No matter how hard you shake the bottle, which liquid will always lay on the top and why?
5. Did you figure out how to get the water and alcohol to trade places with each other?
6. Why did the three liquids always separate themselves?
7. Which liquids mixed together and which did not mix together?

Backyard Scientist solution to experiment.

No matter how hard you shake the oil and water and try to mix them, they just won't mix together. When two liquids will not mix together, the scientific word for this separate state is called immiscible. Did you observe that after you shook the bottle, it was fascinating to look closely and see that the oil had broken into little bits or droplets, but it had not actually mixed with the water? The droplets are suspended in the water. In a little while, the water and oil will separate from each other again. This is called to coalesce, the scientific word for running together. No matter how much you try to mix these two liquids, the oil will always float to the top and lay there. This is because it is the lighter (less dense) of the two liquids.

You have just made a liquid sandwich. In this bottle we have two miscible liquids and one immiscible liquid. The alcohol and water are miscible—that is they will mix with each other. The oil is immiscible and will not mix with either the water or the alcohol. By using the oil to keep the alcohol and water separate, you can, with careful handling, have the water and alcohol trade places. Carefully turn the bottle on its side. This must be done very slowly. Be very careful when you tip the liquid. If you let the oil layer barrier down, the layers of alcohol and water will disappear into each other because they are miscible liquids. After you shake the bottle and let it stand for a while, the oil will separate from the others because the oil is immiscible.

Try making layers with other liquids. Are these other liquids miscible or immiscible?

Exploring the properties of dry ice, frozen carbon dioxide gas (CO_2).

Try the following Backyard Scientist experiment to discover the answer.

**THE FOLLOWING DRY ICE EXPERIMENTS MUST BE DONE WITH AN ADULT.
DRY ICE WILL BURN AND BLISTER THE SKIN IF IT COMES INTO DIRECT CONTACT WITH
THE SKIN. GLOVES MUST ALWAYS BE WORN WHEN HANDLING DRY ICE. REMEMBER,
NEVER DRINK OR EAT ANYTHING YOU ARE EXPERIMENTING WITH UNLESS YOU ARE
INSTRUCTED TO DO SO IN THE EXPERIMENT.**

Gather the following supplies:

Ten pounds or more of dry ice, gloves, (like gardening gloves or rubber dish washing gloves), an
insulated chest to store the dry ice, hot water from the tap, 2 colors of food coloring, two 14 to 16
oz. plastic containers, (tall, narrow ones if available), 1 oz. liquid detergent (any brand), 1 dishpan
or baking pan with sides, and 1 hammer or screwdriver.

Dry ice is available from commercial ice companies. Look in the yellow pages of your telephone
book. Dry ice is packaged in blocks, slices and pellets. Most companies carry it in blocks and will
cut or slice it for you. Pellets do not work as well as slices or blocks. Shop around, prices vary.
Dry ice in an insulated chest or Styrofoam container loses about 5% of its volume each 24 hours.
Place the dry ice in paper bags. Fill the empty space inside the chest with crumpled newspapers
for added insulation. **CAUTION: DO NOT STORE DRY ICE IN A CLOSED CAR OVERNIGHT.** It
is safe to keep dry ice in a car when you are transporting it. You can keep dry ice in your house,
classroom or garage. **DO NOT PUT DRY ICE IN A FREEZER OR REFRIGERATOR.**

Start Experimenting:

1. Fill one plastic container 3/4 full with hot water from the tap.
2. Put in about 12 drops of food coloring (any color you wish) until the water changes to that color.
3. Put on the gloves before you start working with the dry ice. Taking the hammer (have an adult help you) gently break off a piece of dry ice small enough to fit into the opening of your water filled container.
4. Wearing the gloves, drop the piece of dry ice into the water. Be sure to observe what is happening.
5. Take the plastic dishpan and put the other tall plastic container into it.
6. Fill it 3/4 full of hot water from the tap.
7. Using a different color of food coloring, put about 12 drops into the water until the water changes to that color.
8. Put about one tablespoon of liquid detergent into this container.
9. Put on the gloves and have an adult help you break off another piece of dry ice as large as will easily fit into the container. Drop this piece into the container. Observe what is taking place. Pop some of the bubbles.
10. Now again wearing your gloves, take a piece of dry ice, any size, and put it on a table and watch it for a few minutes. Be a careful observer. What is happening? NOTE: Always store the dry ice you are not using in the covered insulated container.

Can you answer the following questions from your observations?

1. When you dropped the piece of dry ice into the container with the water and food coloring, what do you think the substance was that came out of the container?

2. When you dropped the piece of dry ice into the second container with the water, food coloring, and liquid detergent, what do you think made all the bubbles? Did you try popping the bubbles?
3. What do you think would happen if you put a lot of liquid detergent into the container?
4. What do you think dry ice is made of?
5. Do you think dry ice is dangerous to breathe?
6. From your observations, how is dry ice different from the ice cubes in your freezer?
7. Do you know how cold dry ice is?
8. In my instructions at the beginning of this experiment, I told you not to put dry ice in the refrigerator or freezer because it will disappear. Why do you think this would happen?
9. If you are on a picnic, would you rather use ice cubes or dry ice for keeping your food cold? Why?
10. When you put the piece of dry ice on the table and watched it, what do you think was happening?

Backyard Scientist solution to experiment.

Ordinary ice is frozen H_2O (water). When the temperature of ice is raised, it turns into a liquid. Raising the temperature further turns it into a gas called steam. Dry ice is frozen CO_2 (carbon dioxide). When its temperature is raised, it turns directly into an invisible gas. It does not go into a liquid state. This is called sublimation. The tall container of water appears to boil when dry ice is dropped into it. The water's temperature is higher than that of the dry ice. This causes the dry ice to sublimate with such power, that the CO_2 bubbles coming up through the water make the water appear as if it is boiling. The normally invisible CO_2 molecules are saturated (filled up) with H_2O molecules as they pass through the column of water, thus making the CO_2 visible and resembling steam.

43

Continue experimenting on the next page.

Dry ice is so cold that it is always sublimating when it is above the temperature and pressure it takes to remain in its frozen state. This means that dry ice changes from a solid state to a gaseous state without going through the intermediary liquid state passed through by water ice, and many other frozen gases.

This is what you observed as you watched the dry ice on the table. However, the quantity of gas involved is so great, and the blocks are so firmly compressed, that considerable time is required for it to sublimate.

In the second part of the experiment, when you added the liquid detergent to the container, the saturated molecules of H_2O and CO_2 gas were trapped in the soap film. The more liquid detergent you put into the container the stronger the film, and the more soap bubbles you will make. You might want to try this outside, because it does get messy when you use more than one tablespoon of soap.

Dry ice is much colder than the ice cubes in your freezer. This is why you must always wear gloves when handling dry ice. It is safe to breathe CO_2 in a well ventilated area. Carbon dioxide makes up much of the air which you are breathing all the time. Plants convert carbon dioxide into oxygen through a process called photosynthesis. CO_2 is used in fire extinguishers and is also what makes the bubbles in carbonated soft drinks.

The reason dry ice will disappear in the refrigerator or freezer is because the fan inside will make it sublimate more rapidly.

You would probably like to use dry ice on a picnic because it does not leave a mess like ice cubes do when they melt. Dry ice is frozen Carbon Dioxide. When bubbles stop coming out and the gas ceases coming from the containers of water and food coloring, you can plop in another piece of dry ice. If no more bubbles come, then you can add another drop of liquid detergent. It is fun to experiment with the gas and pop the bubbles coming from the containers.

Carbon Dioxide—CO_2—is made up of one carbon atom and two oxygen atoms. Water—H_2O—is made up of two hydrogen atoms and one oxygen atom.

Check the bottom of your container. Did regular ice (the H_2O type) form around the dry ice? If it did, what caused this to happen? I'll give you a hint, water freezes at 32 degrees F. which is a much higher temperature than that of the dry ice.

Save the dry ice for the exciting experiment beginning on the next page.

More Experiments with Dry Ice.

Are the molecules more densely packed when a gas is in its solid form rather than in its gaseous form?

Try the following Backyard Scientist experiment to discover the answer.

THE FOLLOWING DRY ICE EXPERIMENTS MUST BE DONE WITH AN ADULT. DRY ICE WILL BURN AND BLISTER THE SKIN IF YOU TOUCH IT DIRECTLY WITH YOUR HANDS. GLOVES MUST ALWAYS BE WORN WHEN HANDLING DRY ICE. REMEMBER, NEVER DRINK OR EAT ANYTHING YOU ARE EXPERIMENTING WITH UNLESS INSTRUCTED TO DO SO BY AN ADULT.

Gather the following supplies:

4 to 6 quarters, 1 slice of dry ice about 6" x 6" and 1/2" thick, several plastic see through film containers with caps, and a film container that you cannot see through (you can get these at your neighborhood film processing centers, usually at no charge), a hammer or screwdriver, two 6 or 8 oz. plastic cups, tin foil, and a piece of wax paper.

Continue experimenting on the next page.

Start Experimenting:

1. While wearing your gloves, break off about a 6" or 8" square of dry ice with the hammer or screwdriver and set it on the wax paper.
2. Take a few quarters at a time and warm them in your hands by rubbing your hands together. Be sure you are wearing gloves.
3. Now taking the quarters, one at a time, and with your gloves on (have an adult help you with this) place the coins on edge until they stick into the surface of the dry ice.
4. After you have placed about three or four coins into the block of dry ice, watch and observe very carefully what is taking place.
5. Continue placing the quarters into the dry ice and observe what is taking place. During this experiment it must be very quiet so you can hear as well as see what is taking place.
6. When the quarters are done with their performance, carefully take the quarters out of the block of ice and set them on the piece of wax paper to warm up. The quarters, at this point, will be very, very, very cold. You can warm up the quarters again in your gloves and repeat the experiment. Do not touch the cold quarters with your bare hands. Now, before we go on to the next dry ice experiment, answer the following questions.

Can you answer the following questions from your observations?

1. What were the coins doing in the dry ice?
2. What made the noise you heard coming from the block of dry ice with the coins in it?
3. What do you think would happen if you let the coins stay in the dry ice for several hours?

Now let's go on to the next dry ice experiment.

REMEMBER, YOU WILL STILL BE WORKING WITH DRY ICE, SO YOU MUST WEAR GLOVES AND HAVE AN ADULT HELP YOU WITH THIS EXPERIMENT.

1. Wearing your gloves, get another piece of dry ice. With the screwdriver or hammer break the dry ice into very small pieces that will fit into the film containers.
2. Use the plastic cups to store the little pieces until you are ready to use them. You will also need this chopped dry ice for the next dry ice experiment, so chop up enough ice to fill both plastic cups. Keep the cups covered with tin foil to keep moisture in the air from condensing on the frozen CO_2.
3. Now take one of the film containers with its cap and, wearing your gloves, fill it almost to the top with the chopped dry ice. Then quickly put the cap on and set it aside for now. Do the same with a few more of the film containers.
4. Stand back and observe what happens to the film containers.
5. You may repeat this a couple of more times and watch what happens very carefully. You can time the events with a watch if you want to.
6. When you are done with this experiment, you can dump the remaining dry ice back into the plastic cups, or leave it in the film containers with their caps off. Watch them to see what will happen.

Can you answer the following questions from your observations?

1. What took place when you put the chopped dry ice into the film containers and put on the caps?
2. Did you also observe something happening to the outside walls of the film containers themselves?

Continue experimenting on the next page.

3. What is the substance that has accumulated all around the outside of the film containers?
4. What made the cap fly off the film container? If you were to put the cap on a film container without dry ice in it, would the cap also fly off?

Backyard Scientist solution to experiment.

Did you discover when you placed the quarters on the dry ice, the quarters began vibrating and made a sound? The reason the quarters wiggle and sing is because they are heating the dry ice very rapidly. As the dry ice is heated, it sublimates and turns directly into its gaseous state. The noise you hear is the dry ice, frozen CO_2 (carbon dioxide) rapidly changing to a gas. If you allowed the quarters to stay in the dry ice, the quarters would freeze into the dry ice as their temperature decreased close to that of the dry ice itself. Did you discover that when you put the chopped dry ice into the film containers and capped them, their tops soon popped up into the air? This happens when frozen CO_2 is placed into a sealed non-expanding container, and when its temperature is raised it causes the pressure inside the container to increase, thus making the cap fly off. Never put dry ice into any completely sealed container. **NEVER PUT FROZEN CO_2 (DRY ICE) INTO A GLASS BOTTLE AND CAP IT, BECAUSE IT WILL EXPLODE AND THE GLASS COULD SHATTER AND HURT YOU.** Did you also notice a white substance forming on the outside of the film caps? This is caused by the moisture in the air being cooled by the cold surface of the container. This process is called condensation. There is an exciting condensation experiment in "The Original Backyard Scientist" book.

The reason frozen CO_2 is called dry ice is because it sublimates and leaves no residue or moisture. It is often used for keeping ice cream and other perishable products from spoiling. Many people who take perishables when traveling will use dry ice. It is also used to keep human organs cold when being shipped from hospital to hospital for organ transplant operations. Did you know that CO_2 cannot exist as a liquid, except at a pressure of more than one thousand pounds per square inch, and at a very low temperature?

Now turn the page for another exciting dry ice experiment. You will need the chopped dry ice which you used in this experiment.

More dry ice experiments.

What would happen if you put chopped dry ice into a balloon?

Try the following Backyard Scientist experiment to discover the answer.

REMEMBER, YOU WILL STILL BE WORKING WITH DRY ICE, SO YOU MUST WEAR GLOVES AND HAVE AN ADULT HELP YOU WITH THIS EXPERIMENT.

Gather the following supplies:

One block of dry ice about 6" square and 1/2" thick, a hammer or screwdriver, two 6 or 8 ounce narrow neck plastic containers, several plastic spoons, a watch with a second hand, protective gloves (the kind you used in the preceding experiment), a small funnel and several 8" or 9" balloons. Also use the chopped dry ice from the previous experiment, 1 plastic bottle from 8 to 12 ounces may be used **(GLASS MAY NOT BE SUBSTITUTED UNDER ANY CONDITIONS)**, and one balloon filled with helium, if available.

Start Experimenting:

REMEMBER, YOU ARE STILL WORKING WITH DRY ICE, SO YOU MUST WEAR GLOVES AND HAVE AN ADULT HELP WITH THIS EXPERIMENT.

1. Take one of the balloons and stretch it several times, then insert the narrow end of the funnel into the mouth of the balloon. Wearing your gloves, and having an adult help you, put about ten to twelve pieces of the chopped dry ice into the balloon. You will have to push the dry ice

pieces through the funnel and down into the balloon with the handle of the spoon. Carefully remove the funnel and tie a knot in the balloon. Observe what is happening to the balloon. At this point, you may take off your gloves and feel the outside of the balloon. You may hold it in your hands and watch and feel what is happening right before your eyes. The dry ice in the balloon will not harm you, because the rubber of the balloon will protect your hands from the cold.

2. Wearing the rubber gloves again, fill several of the other balloons with different amounts of dry ice. Always wear your gloves and always have an adult help you when working with dry ice. Do not put more than twenty pieces of dry ice into any balloon. Keep track of how many pieces of dry ice you are putting into each balloon. You might want to make a chart for this. Using different color balloons will help you keep track more easily.

3. Now, take another balloon and blow it up with your mouth to the same diameter as one of the dry ice balloons. Drop both balloons from the same height at the same time. Compare how long it takes the two to reach the floor.

4. If you can get a balloon filled with helium, you might release all three balloons from the same height to see how long it takes for each one to reach the ground.

5. Fill the plastic bottle with some chopped dry ice (about 1 cup). Put a tight fitting balloon over the top of the plastic bottle and watch what happens. **NEVER USE A GLASS BOTTLE FOR THIS EXPERIMENT. YOU MUST ALWAYS USE A PLASTIC BOTTLE.**

Can you answer the following questions from your observations?

1. What happened to the balloons?
2. Did the amount of dry ice you put into the balloons affect their size?
3. Could a balloon explode if you were to put too many pieces of dry ice into it?
4. Which balloon hit the ground first—was it the balloon with dry ice in it or the balloon you blew up with your mouth?

5. If you add a balloon filled with helium to the other two balloons, and release them from the same height, which balloon would hit the ground first, second, or third? Could you get any of these balloons to float in the air?
6. What happened to the balloon on the plastic bottle filled with dry ice?

Backyard Scientist solution to experiment.

Did you observe that when you put pieces of dry ice into the balloon, the balloon inflated? This occurred because the dry ice sublimated as it warmed, turning into CO_2 gas which caused the balloon to expand. As a gas is warmed, it expands and becomes less dense. The more pieces of dry ice you put into the balloon the bigger it got. If you put more pieces of dry ice than instructed into the balloon, it might pop. However, if you use a larger balloon (greater volume), you can put more dry ice into it.

If you dropped the balloon with the dry ice and the balloon with your own air, the balloon filled with the CO_2 fell faster because, despite the equal volumes, it was heavier. CO_2 is more dense than the air we breathe. If you let loose of the helium balloon, it floated up into the air. Helium is used in balloons because of its relatively low density. The combination of the helium and the balloon weigh less than the air which they displaced, so the helium filled balloon floated in the air.

There is one last experiment on the following page using dry ice and an aquarium for learning a completely new concept. The dry ice/aquarium experiment is also great to do at a party.

Can you make soap bubbles float on a cushion of carbon dioxide gas?

Try the following Backyard Scientist experiment to discover the answer.

Gather the following supplies:

One small glass aquarium (about 16-1/2" long x 8-1/2" wide x 11" deep (the dimensions can vary), 1 slab of dry ice about 6" x 6" x 1/2", bubble solution, (you can make your own using the formula in "The Original Backyard Scientist"), gloves, a comb and some wool, or something made of wool. This experiment is fun to do with your family, class, or at any kind of group event.

THE FOLLOWING DRY ICE EXPERIMENTS MUST BE DONE WITH AN ADULT. DRY ICE WILL BURN AND BLISTER THE SKIN IF YOU TOUCH IT DIRECTLY WITH YOUR HANDS. GLOVES MUST ALWAYS BE WORN WHEN HANDLING DRY ICE. REMEMBER, NEVER DRINK OR EAT ANYTHING YOU ARE EXPERIMENTING WITH UNLESS INSTRUCTED TO DO SO BY AN ADULT.

Start Experimenting:

1. Place the aquarium on a table or counter top where it is at a comfortable height to do your experiment. Wearing your gloves, place a slab of dry ice (frozen CO_2) flat in the bottom of the aquarium. Allow about fifteen minutes for a layer of carbon dioxide gas to accumulate. For best results, this should be done inside the house in an area with still air and away from any heater or air conditioning vents.

2. Using the bubble solution and a wand, gently blow bubbles into the aquarium so the bubbles float down into the aquarium. For best results stand slightly back from the aquarium and do not blow the bubbles directly into it.

3. As you are blowing the bubbles into the aquarium, carefully observe what is happening. It might take a little practice to blow the bubbles very gently so they just float down into the aquarium.

4. Watch very carefully as the bubbles descend and then float on the denser layer of carbon dioxide gas in the lower part of the aquarium. They may even bounce up a little after floating down onto the CO_2 gas. Keep watching and observe very carefully for about five minutes.

5. Observe what happens when several bubbles are floating around as compared to only one.

6. Now rub the comb on the wool to charge the comb with static electricity.
7. Put the comb near the bubbles, but don't touch the bubbles with the comb. See how the bubbles respond to the comb.

Can you answer the following questions from your observations?

1. After the bubbles descended, why did they seem to float in mid-air and usually at about the same level?
2. Did you see different colors in the bubbles? Why?
3. What did you observe as the bubbles hit the dry ice?
4. What did you observe when blowing several bubbles into the aquarium at one time?
5. How did the bubbles respond to the charged comb?
6. Do you think the bubbles that floated inside the aquarium are filled with air or carbon dioxide?
7. Why didn't the bubbles contract when cooled by the dry ice?

Backyard Scientist solution to experiment.

The bubbles will actually appear to float in mid-air from one to several inches above the bottom of the aquarium. Notice how the bubbles begin to expand, and then sink to the bottom, and then freeze onto the dry ice. What is actually taking place is that the dry ice sublimates or turns into CO_2 gas. CO_2 gas is denser than the air inside the aquarium, and it replaces the air at the bottom of the aquarium, forming a layer at the bottom. A bubble full of air floats on the carbon dioxide layer just like a helium balloon will float in the air.

The bubble did not cool and contract near the dry ice. Instead the bubble actually expanded slightly. This took place because the soapy wall of the bubble allows CO_2 molecules to pass into the bubble, but does not allow air molecules to pass out of the bubble. Initially, the concentration of CO_2 gas is low inside the bubble and high outside the bubble. The gas gradually diffuses into the bubble. This process is called osmosis. The bubble film is a semi-permeable membrane—a material that allows some substances to pass through while preventing others from passing through. Your cells have the same property. Oxygen and CO_2 easily enter some cells, while other molecules do not. The added CO_2 makes the bubble denser, causing it to gradually sink. The frozen CO_2, at the bottom of the tank, is cold enough to freeze the bubble.

When you blew several bubbles into the aquarium, did you notice that the bubbles of different sizes collided with each other? Sometimes they join as two or more bubbles with a flat or bulging wall between them. A flat wall forms between two bubbles of equal size. The wall bulges away from the smaller of two bubbles because smaller bubbles have higher pressure inside them.

Did you notice that when you put the charged comb over the bubbles, the electrically neutral bubbles were electrically polarized by, and attracted to, the charged comb? This type of electrical charge is called static electricity (more about static electricity is in "Backyard Scientist, Series One").

The different colors you saw in the bubbles were caused by the refraction of light. For more on this subject see "The Original Backyard Scientist."

EXTRAS...

Get your official Backyard Scientist Certificate and join the Backyard Scientist Club! Just print your name on a slip of paper and state that you have completed all the experiments in the book. Be sure to enclose first class postage, and I will send you your official Backyard Scientist Certificate and enroll you in the Backyard Scientist Club. Also, The Backyard Scientist would like to know which experiments you liked best and why. Write to: **Backyard Scientist, P. O. Box 16966, Irvine, CA 92713.**

GET READY FOR MORE ADVENTURES WITH HANDS-ON SCIENCE EXPERIMENTS IN:

"Backyard Scientist, Series Two"
Experiments for
Ages 9 through 14 years

"The Original Backyard Scientist"
Experiments for
Ages 4 through 12 years

This is the author's first book and it features many of the author's most popular experiments.

This is the author's third book featuring a special collection of exciting, fascinating and challenging experiments for children ages 9 through 14 years.

"Backyard Scientist, Series One"
Experiments for
Ages 4 through 12 years

"Backyard Scientist, Series Three"
Experiments in the Life Sciences for
Ages 4 through 12

This is the author's second book of fascinating and fun ways to explore the world of science.

The fourth book in the series contains challenging, yet easy to understand experiments in the life sciences, including: biology, entomology, physiology and more.

Backyard Scientist books are available from many bookstores, school supply stores, museum shops and toy stores. Or, you can order by mail from: **Backyard Scientist, P. O. Box 16966, Irvine, CA 92713.** Include your check or money order for $9.50 (includes shipping and handling) for each book ordered. California residents add sales tax.